Soonerology Trivia Challenge

Oklahoma Sooners Football

Soonerology Trivia Challenge – Oklahoma Sooners Football;
First Edition 2008

Published by
Kick The Ball, Ltd
8595 Columbus Pike, Suite 197
Lewis Center, OH 43035
www.TriviaGameBooks.com

Designed, Formatted, and Edited by: Paul F. Wilson & Tom P. Rippey III
Researched by: Paul F. Wilson

For information on ordering this book in bulk at reduced prices, please email us
at pfwilson@trivianthology.com.

International Standard Book Number: 978-1-934372-43-2

Printed & Bound in the United States of America

Paul F. Wilson & Tom P. Rippey III

Soonerology Trivia Challenge

Oklahoma Sooners Football

Researched by Paul F. Wilson

Paul F. Wilson & Tom P. Rippey III, Editors

Kick The Ball, Ltd
Lewis Center, Ohio

This book is dedicated to our families and friends for your unwavering love, support, and your understanding of our pursuit of our passions. Thank you for everything you do for us and for making our lives complete.

Dear Friend,

Thank you for purchasing our *Soonerology Trivia Challenge* game book!

We hope you enjoy it as much as we enjoyed researching and putting it together. This book can be used over and over again in many different ways. One example would be to use it in a head-to-head challenge by alternating questions between Sooner football fans – or by playing as teams. Another option would be to simply challenge yourself to see how many questions you could answer correctly. No matter how you choose to use this book, you'll have fun and maybe even learn a fact or two about Sooners football.

We have made every attempt to verify the accuracy of the questions and answers contained in this book. However it is still possible that from time to time an error has been made by us or our researchers. In the event you find a question or answer that is questionable or inaccurate, we ask for your understanding and thank you for bringing it to our attention so that we may improve future editions of this book. Please email us at tprippey@trivianthology.com with those observations and comments.

Have fun playing *Soonerology Trivia Challenge*!

Paul & Tom

Paul Wilson & Tom Rippey
Co-Founders, Kick The Ball, Ltd

PS – You can discover more about all of our current trivia game books by visiting us online at www.TriviaGameBooks.com.

Table of Contents

How to Play

Book Format:

There are four quarters, each made up of fifty questions. Each quarter's questions have assigned point values. Questions are designed to get progressively more difficult as you proceed through each quarter, as well as through the book itself. Most questions are in a four-option multiple-choice format so that you will at least have a 25% chance of getting a correct answer for some of the more challenging questions.

We've even added an *Overtime* section in the event of a tie, or just in case you want to keep playing a little longer.

Game Options:

One Player -
To play on your own, simply answer each of the questions in all the quarters, and in the overtime section, if you'd like. Use the *Player / Team Score Sheet* to record your answers and the quarter *Answer Keys* to check your answers. Calculate each quarter's points and the total for the game at the bottom of the *Player / Team Score Sheet* to determine your final score.

Two or More Players –
To play with multiple players decide if you will all be competing with each other individually, or if you will form and play as teams. Each player / team will then have its own *Player / Team Score Sheet* to record its answer. You can use the quarter *Answer Keys* to check your answers and to calculate your final scores.

1

The *Player / Team Score Sheets* have been designed so that each team can answer all questions or you can divide the questions up in any combination you would prefer. For example, you may want to alternate questions if two players are playing or answer every third question for three players, etc. In any case, simply record your response to your questions in the corresponding quarter and question number on the *Player / Team Score Sheet*.

A winner will be determined by multiplying the total number of correct answers for each quarter by the point value per quarter, then adding together the final total for all quarters combined. Play the game again and again by alternating the questions that your team is assigned so that you will answer a different set of questions each time you play.

You Create the Game -
There are countless other ways of using *Soonerology Trivia Challenge* questions. It's limited only to your imagination. Examples might be using them at your tailgate or other college football related party. Players / Teams who answer questions incorrectly may have to perform a required action, or winners may receive special prizes. Let us know what other games you come up with!

Have fun!

1) What year did Oklahoma officially adopt the nickname "Sooners" for the school's athletics?

    A) 1893
    B) 1898
    C) 1908
    D) 1913

2) What are the official colors for the Sooners?

    A) Crimson & White
    B) Red & Cream
    C) Scarlet & White
    D) Crimson & Cream

3) Oklahoma's stadium has a seating capacity of over 80,000.

    A) True
    B) False

4) What year did Oklahoma play its first game?

    A) 1881
    B) 1890
    C) 1895
    D) 1901

First Quarter

SOONEROLOGY TRIVIA CHALLENGE

5) What is one of the most recognizable college football traditions performed by the Oklahoma marching band?

A) The "OU" Shuffle
B) Interlocking "OU" March
C) "OU" Reverse Script
D) Pride of Oklahoma Walk

6) In which state was Sooners Coach Bob Stoops born?

A) Ohio
B) Oklahoma
C) Oregon
D) California

7) In the lyrics of the Oklahoma fight song, how many times is the word "Sooner" used?

A) 5
B) 7
C) 8
D) 10

8) Which Sooners head coach had the longest tenure?

A) Bennie Owen
B) Barry Switzer
C) Charles "Bud" Wilkinson
D) Vernon Parrington

OKLAHOMA SOONERS FOOTBALL

9) Who was the first player from Oklahoma to be picked number one overall in the NFL Draft?

    A)   Billy Sims
    B)   Lee Roy Selmon
    C)   Dave Baker
    D)   Max Boydston

10) What is the name of the trophy kept by the winner of the Red River Shootout?

    A)   Red River Victors Cup
    B)   Golden Cup
    C)   Golden Hat
    D)   The Reddie

11) How many Heisman trophies have been won by Oklahoma players?

    A)   1
    B)   2
    C)   3
    D)   4

12) Does Oklahoma have an all-time winning record against Nebraska?

    A)   Yes
    B)   No

13) What is the name of Oklahoma's official mascot?

A) Boomer Schooner
B) Land Runner
C) Sooner Schooner
D) Sooner Boomer

14) In which year did the term "Sooner Magic" originate?

A) 1967
B) 1976
C) 1986
D) 1997

15) What is the name of the stadium where the Sooners play?

A) Norman Memorial Stadium
B) Grace Family – Memorial Football Stadium
C) Gaylord Family – Oklahoma Memorial Stadium
D) Oklahoma Sooner Outdoor Stadium

16) In which year was the first undefeated season for Oklahoma (minimum 8 games)?

A) 1911
B) 1915
C) 1916
D) 1921

First Quarter

1-Point Questions

17) What is written across the Sooner Schooner's canvas cover?

- A) Interlocking "OU"
- B) Oklahoma Sooners
- C) Sooners
- D) Sooner Schooner

18) In a pregame ritual, Pride of Oklahoma trombone players touch a concrete beam inscribed with what?

- A) Win
- B) Pride
- C) Victory
- D) Oklahoma

19) Who holds the career rushing record at Oklahoma?

- A) Adrian Peterson
- B) Billy Sims
- C) Steve Owens
- D) Darrell Shepard

20) Who was the Sooners' first consensus All-American?

- A) Buddy Burris
- B) Claude Reeds
- C) Roland "Waddy" Young
- D) Forest "Spot" Geyer

21) For how many yards was Adrian Peterson's first TD
rush at Oklahoma?

    A) 15
    B) 35
    C) 55
    D) 75

22) What is inscribed on the traditional locker room sign
that OU players touch before taking the field?

    A) Fight Oklahoma Fight!
    B) Sooner Pride
    C) Win Together
    D) Play Like A Champion Today

23) Which OU coach has the most wins as a Sooner?

    A) Bud Wilkinson
    B) Bennie Owen
    C) Barry Switzer
    D) Bob Stoops

24) What year did Oklahoma join the Southwest
Conference (SWC)?

    A) 1907
    B) 1914
    C) 1921
    D) 1928

25) Who holds the record for passing yards in a single game at Oklahoma?

    A) Cale Gundy
    B) Sam Bradford
    C) Jason White
    D) Josh Heupel

26) How many offensive returning starters does Oklahoma have in 2008?

    A) 8
    B) 9
    C) 10
    D) 11

27) Against which U.S. Service Academy is OU undefeated?

    A) Air Force
    B) Army
    C) Navy
    D) OU has lost to each of the academies

28) What shape are the helmet stickers OU players receive for outstanding plays?

    A) Interlocking "OU" logo
    B) State of Oklahoma
    C) Outline of the Sooner Schooner
    D) Helmet stickers are not awarded to players

29) Have Oklahoma and Nebraska ever played on a neutral site?

A) Yes
B) No

30) Who holds the Oklahoma record for career victories by a quarterback?

A) Jason White
B) Josh Heupel
C) Steve Davis
D) Eddie Crowder

31) Who led the Sooners in sacks in 2007?

A) Auston English
B) Nic Harris
C) DeMarcus Granger
D) Alonzo Dotson

32) Which team has Oklahoma played the most in bowl games?

A) Alabama
B) Arkansas
C) Florida State
D) LSU

33) Who has received the most individual national awards while at Oklahoma?

    A) Billy Sims
    B) Jason White
    C) Brian Bosworth
    D) Lee Roy Selmon

34) In which of the following categories did OU not lead the Big 12 in 2007?

    A) Red Zone Defense
    B) Sacks By
    C) Kickoff Returns
    D) Field Goals

35) Which former player is currently the OU QBs coach?

    A) Josh Heupel
    B) Cale Gundy
    C) Jackie Shipp
    D) None of the above

36) Who was the first 2-time consensus All-American for Oklahoma?

    A) Buddy Burris
    B) Jim Weatherall
    C) Wade Walker
    D) Frank "Pop" Ivy

37) What's the nickname of the annual rivalry game played between OU and Oklahoma State?

    A) Beckham Series
    B) Mayhem Rivalry Game
    C) Bedlam Football Game
    D) Medley Football Game

38) What are the most games the Sooners have won at home in single season?

    A) 7
    B) 8
    C) 9
    D) None of the above

39) What is the name of the Oklahoma fight song?

    A) Oklahoma!
    B) Boomer Sooner
    C) The OU Chant
    D) Fight for OKU

40) What is the name of the sports facility located at the south end of Memorial Stadium?

    A) Barry Switzer Athletic Union
    B) Bennie Owen Center
    C) Gaylord Family Center
    D) Barry Switzer Center

41) How many *AP* National Championships has Oklahoma been awarded?

- A) 6
- B) 7
- C) 9
- D) 13

42) Who holds the Oklahoma record for receiving yards in a season?

- A) Antwone Savage
- B) Keith Jackson
- C) Mark Clayton
- D) Buster Rhymes

43) What is the shape of the trophy awarded to the winner of the Bedlam game?

- A) Bell
- B) State of Oklahoma
- C) Football Helmet
- D) Arch

44) How many Big 12 Championships has Oklahoma won?

- A) 2
- B) 3
- C) 5
- D) 7

45) Which player holds the single game rushing record at Oklahoma?

    A) De'Mond Parker
    B) Greg Pruitt
    C) Billy Sims
    D) Mike Gaddis

46) Who was the first consensus All-American quarterback for Oklahoma?

    A) Jason White
    B) Jack Mildren
    C) Eddie Crowder
    D) Josh Heupel

47) How many OU head coaches lasted just one season?

    A) 3
    B) 6
    C) 10
    D) None of them

48) What award did Sooner offensive tackle Jammal Brown win in 2007?

    A) Outland Trophy
    B) Thorpe Award
    C) Bednarik Award
    D) Lombardi Award

49) Who holds the Oklahoma career record for points scored?

    A) R.D. Lashar
    B) Steve Owens
    C) Billy Sims
    D) Quentin Griffin

50) In which year did the Sooners first celebrate a victory over Nebraska?

    A) 1912
    B) 1915
    C) 1924
    D) 1930

First Quarter Sooner Cool Fact

Roland "Waddy" Young was not merely an All-American, he was a true American hero. A gifted athlete and fierce competitor, Waddy dominated the gridiron, the wrestling mat, and the boxing ring too. A two-way football player, Waddy anchored one of the Sooners' stingiest defenses of all time, which allowed a mere 12 points the entire 1938 season. Following two seasons with the NFL's Brooklyn Dodgers Waddy enlisted in the Army Air Corps to do his part to end World War II. A B-29 pilot, Waddy took part in the first Tokyo raid launched from Saipan in November of 1944. Two short months later, his squadron would find itself under heavy attack as it made its way back to base. Waddy fell back to help another pilot in need when his plane would forever disappear amidst the fighting. Fittingly, his final words were said to be *"We are OK."*

First Quarter Answer Key

1) C – 1908 (They were known as Boomers or Rough Riders prior to the official adoption of Sooners.)

2) D – Crimson & Cream (Chosen in 1895 by a committee established to select the school's official colors.)

3) A – True (The Stadium's official seating capacity is 82,112.)

4) C – 1895 (The game was played on November 7th of that year.)

5) B – Interlocking "OU" March (The band plays the OU fight song while marching down the field in this celebrated formation.)

6) A – Ohio (Coach Stoops was born in Youngstown, Ohio on September 9, 1960.)

7) D – 10 (The word "Oklahoma" is also used 10 times in the Lyrics.)

8) A – Bennie Owen (Coach Owen led the Sooners 22 seasons from 1905-1926.)

9) B – Lee Roy Selmon (Drafted #1 overall by the Buccaneers in 1976.)

10) C – Golden Hat (The trophy, a gold ten-gallon hat, is safeguarded by the winning team's athletic department.)

11) D – 4 (Billy Vessels in 1952, Steve Owens in 1969, Billy Sims in 1978, and Jason White in 2003)

12) A – Yes (The Sooners lead the series 43-37-3 [.536].)

13) C – Sooner Schooner (A replica Conestoga wagon pulled by white ponies named Boomer and Sooner.)

14) B – 1976 (A stunning come-from-behind victory over Nebraska in Lincoln led to the first use of the term that would eventually characterize other magical fourth-quarter comebacks over the Huskers.)

15) C – Gaylord Family – Oklahoma Memorial Stadium (Dating back to 1923, the stadium's ever-changing features are a hallmark of OU's campus.)

16) A – 1911 (The Sooners ended that season 8-0.)

17) D – Sooner Schooner (Crimson letters on white canvas)

18) B – Pride (A tradition performed while waiting in the stadium tunnel prior to taking the field at home games.)

19) B – Billy Sims (Billy totaled 4,118 yards from 1975-79.)

20) C – Roland "Waddy" Young (1938)

21) B – 35 (Peterson rushed for 100 yards including a 35-yard touchdown in his OU debut versus Bowling Green.)

22) D – Play Like A Champion Today (Although more popularly associated with Notre Dame, this sign is a long-time Oklahoma tradition.)

23) C – Barry Switzer (From 1973-88 Coach Switzer was 157-29-4, winning 100 conference games along the way.)

24) B – 1914 (OU was a charter member along with 7 other members from the states of Arkansas, Oklahoma, and Texas.)

25) D – Josh Heupel (429 yards in 1999 at Louisville)

26) A – 8 (Sam Bradford, Branndon Braxton, Jon Cooper, Juaquin Iglesias, Manuel Johnson, Phil Loadholt, Duke Robinson, and Brandon Walker)

27) A – Air Force (OU is 1-0 versus Air Force; OU 44, Air Force 3 on September 1, 2001.)

28) D – Helmet stickers are not awarded to players

29) A – Yes (Games have been played in Omaha, NE; Oklahoma City, OK; and Miami, FL.)

30) C – Steve Davis (Steve leads all OU quarterbacks with 32 victories from 1973-75.)

31) A – Auston English (9.5 sacks for 64 yards lost)

32) C – Florida State (OU has played Florida State four times for a bowl record of 3-1 vs. the Seminoles.)

33) B – Jason White (2003 Heisman Trophy, 2004 Unitas Award, 2004 Maxwell Award, and the 2003 & 2004 Davey O'Brien Awards)

34) D – Field Goals (Of the categories listed, the only one in which OU did not lead the Big 12 in 2007 was Field Goals – for which OU was 2nd behind Nebraska.)

35) A – Josh Heupel (2005-present)

36) B – Jim Weatherall (1950 and 1951)

37) C – Bedlam Football Game (OU leads the series with an overall record of 78-16-7 [.807].)

38) A – 7 (7-0 in 2007 and 7-0 in 2003 at home)

39) B – Boomer Sooner (Written by a student in 1905.)

40) D – Barry Switzer Center (Dedicated in 1999, it houses locker & equipment rooms, coaches offices, sports medicine center, and the Touchdown Club Legends lobby.)

41) B – 7 (1950, 1955, 1956, 1974, 1975, 1985, & 2000)

42) C – Mark Clayton (In 2003 Mark had 1,425 yards receiving.)

43) A – Bell (The Bedlam Bell is a crystal trophy modeled after Oklahoma State's Old Central's bell clapper.)

44) C – 5 (Since its formation, OU has earned 5 Big 12 titles in 2000, 2002, 2004, 2006, & 2007.)

45) B – Greg Pruitt (294 yards at Kansas State in 1971)

46) D – Josh Heupel (Consensus All-American in 2000)

47) B – 6 (Jack Harts, Fred Roberts, Fred Ewing, Jim Tatum, Jim Mackenzie, and Howard Schnellenberger)

48) A – Outland Trophy (Presented annually to the nation's most outstanding lineman.)

49) B – Steve Owens (From 1967-69 Steve scored 342 points for OU.)

50) C – 1924 (OU did not secure its 1st win in the series until the teams' 6th matchup; OU 14, Nebraska 7.)

Note: All answers valid as of the end of the 2007 season, unless otherwise indicated in the question itself.

Second Quarter *2-Point Questions*

1) What is the name of the pre-game family-friendly event held on the OU campus before each home game?

    A) Sooner Fan Fest
    B) Sooner Fun Fest
    C) Sooner Game Day Fest
    D) Sooner Family Fun Fest

2) What number did Sooner great Brian Bosworth wear?

    A) 33
    B) 34
    C) 40
    D) 44

3) How many OU defensive players are in the College Football Hall of Fame?

    A) 0
    B) 2
    C) 5
    D) 7

4) In how many different decades have the Sooners won at least 85 games?

    A) 0
    B) 2
    C) 4
    D) 7

5) Has any other team played in more BCS title games than Oklahoma?

    A) Yes
    B) No

6) How many times has Oklahoma finished the season undefeated?

    A) 5
    B) 8
    C) 11
    D) 14

7) When was the first time the Sooners traveled out-of-state for a game?

    A) 1898
    B) 1901
    C) 1907
    D) 1912

8) Which U.S. Service Academy has Oklahoma never played?

    A) Air Force
    B) Navy
    C) Army
    D) OU has played all three

9) The Sooners' Brian Bosworth is the only college football player to win two Butkus Awards.

    A) True
    B) False

10) Which school has Oklahoma played LESS THAN 75 times?

    A) Texas
    B) Iowa State
    C) Oklahoma State
    D) Nebraska

11) What is Oklahoma's winning percentage against Texas?

    A) .417
    B) .512
    C) .631
    D) .637

12) Who holds the Oklahoma record for most passing yards in a single game against Nebraska?

    A) Sam Bradford
    B) Josh Heupel
    C) Jason White
    D) Cale Gundy

13) How many times has Oklahoma hosted ESPN's *College Gameday*?

    A) 3
    B) 5
    C) 7
    D) 9

14) What year was the first winning season at Oklahoma?

    A) 1896
    B) 1901
    C) 1904
    D) 1905

15) What is the record for most points scored by Oklahoma against Texas?

    A) 52
    B) 63
    C) 65
    D) 77

16) Which Oklahoma running back holds the Big 12 freshman record for rushing yards?

    A) De'Mond Parker
    B) Kejuan Jones
    C) Quentin Griffin
    D) Adrian Peterson

17) What are the most consecutive wins OU has had over rival Nebraska?

    A) 11
    B) 16
    C) 19
    D) 22

18) What is the Sooners' all-time record against Baylor?

    A) 13-4
    B) 15-2
    C) 17-0
    D) None of the above

19) How many Oklahoma players have been selected number one overall in the NFL Draft?

    A) 0
    B) 2
    C) 3
    D) 6

20) The Sooners have won more than 20 bowl games.

    A) True
    B) False

21) For how many yards was the longest rushing play in Oklahoma history?

- A) 87 yards
- B) 89 yards
- C) 96 yards
- D) 100 yards

22) In which bowl was Oklahoma's first bowl appearance?

- A) Gator Bowl
- B) Orange Bowl
- C) Sugar Bowl
- D) Bluebonnet Bowl

23) Sooner Jack Mildren received all of the following Academic honors EXCEPT?

- A) Rhodes Scholar
- B) NFF Scholar Athlete
- C) Academic All-American
- D) Academic All-American Hall of Fame

24) How many times has Oklahoma appeared in the Orange Bowl?

- A) 3
- B) 4
- C) 6
- D) 18

25) How many times has a Sooner finished second in Heisman voting?

A) 0
B) 2
C) 5
D) 7

26) What year did Oklahoma win its first Big 8 title?

A) 1959
B) 1979
C) 1987
D) 1996

27) How many times has Oklahoma been ranked number one in the Preseason *AP* poll?

A) 5
B) 6
C) 9
D) 10

28) Oklahoma has the most 10+ win seasons of any major college football program.

A) True
B) False

29) Who was the Oklahoma head coach in its first season of football?

   A) Adrian Lindsey
   B) Fred Roberts
   C) Jack Harts
   D) No coach

30) How many games did Oklahoma play in its first season?

   A) 1
   B) 2
   C) 3
   D) 5

31) Who owns the Oklahoma record for most receiving yards in a single game against Nebraska?

   A) Mark Clayton
   B) Ben Hart
   C) Tinker Owens
   D) Malcolm Kelly

32) What are the most points the Sooners have scored in the first half of play?

   A) 52 points
   B) 59 points
   C) 71 points
   D) 73 points

33) Who has the most rushing yards for Oklahoma in a single game against Texas?

A) Billy Sims
B) Greg Pruitt
C) De'Mond Parker
D) Adrian Peterson

34) What is OU's all-time largest margin of victory?

A) 157 points
B) 179 points
C) 184 points
D) 188 points

35) Which team did Oklahoma suffer its worst loss (margin of loss) to in the 2007 season?

A) Miami
B) Texas Tech
C) Colorado
D) West Virginia

36) Who was Oklahoma's first opponent in Memorial Stadium?

A) Washington
B) Texas Tech
C) Baylor
D) Oklahoma State

37) Since its inception in 1985, how many times have Sooners won the Butkus Award?

  A) 1
  B) 2
  C) 4
  D) 5

38) How many total consensus All-Americans has OU had?

  A) 51
  B) 63
  C) 72
  D) 84

39) Who holds the Oklahoma record for passing yards in a season?

  A) Jason White
  B) Sam Bradford
  C) Josh Heupel
  D) Paul Thomspon

40) Oklahoma is the only Big 12 School to have had a quarterback win the Heisman trophy.

  A) True
  B) False

SOONEROLOGY TRIVIA CHALLENGE

41) Who holds the OU single game receiving yards record?

    A) Corey Warren
    B) Mark Clayton
    C) Ben Hart
    D) Eddie Hinton

42) How many Sooner players have had over 1,000 yards rushing in a single season?

    A) 13
    B) 17
    C) 26
    D) 31

43) Who was the first consensus All-American defensive back at Oklahoma?

    A) Zac Henderson
    B) Randy Hughes
    C) Ricky Dixon
    D) None of the above

44) How many conference Championships has Oklahoma won?

    A) 26
    B) 31
    C) 37
    D) 41

OKLAHOMA SOONERS FOOTBALL

45) How many jersey numbers has OU retired?

    A) 1
    B) 4
    C) 8
    D) None of the above

46) What is OU's home record under Coach Stoops?

    A) 54-2
    B) 55-5
    C) 57-8
    D) 61-13

47) How many Sooners football players are in the Oklahoma Sports Hall of Fame?

    A) 7
    B) 9
    C) 13
    D) 18

48) How many times in his career has Coach Stoops won National Coach of the Year?

    A) 0
    B) 1
    C) 2
    D) 4

49) What decade did Oklahoma have the best winning percentage?

    A) 1950s
    B) 1970s
    C) 2000s
    D) None of the above

50) How many Oklahoma players have won Orange Bowl MVP?

    A) 9
    B) 14
    C) 17
    D) 24

Second Quarter Sooner Cool Fact

With an overall record in the decade of 93-10-2, including an unparalleled 47-game winning streak, Coach Bud Wilkinson's Sooners were nothing short of sensational throughout the 1950s. Along the way, he and his teams set two NCAA FBS (Division 1-A at the time) records that have endured the years despite the threat from many other dominate coaches and teams throughout college football since that decade. These records include the all-time highest decade-long winning percentage of .895 and of course the 47-game winning streak. Whether these records are broken someday or not, Coach Wilkinson will always be remembered for laying the foundation for the winningest college football program of the modern era.

Second Quarter Answer Key

1) A – Sooner Fan Fest (The event opens three hours prior to the game and ends when the Pride of Oklahoma marches into the stadium before kickoff.)

2) D – 44 (The Bos wore number 44 while at Oklahoma and number 55 for the two years he played for the Seattle Seahawks.)

3) B – 2 (Sooners Lee Roy Selmon & Tony Casillas were inducted for primary defensive positions.)

4) C – 4 (OU's total wins for each of these decades surpassed 85: 93 wins in the 1950s, 102 wins in the 1970s, 91 wins in the 1980s, & 90 wins up to this point in the 2000s.)

5) B – No (Oklahoma, Ohio State, and Florida State are all tied in both their number of Championship Game appearances [3] and their overall records [1-2] in those games.)

6) D – 14 (The Sooners were undefeated at the end of each of the following seasons: 1896-98, 1911, 1915, 1918, 1920, 1949, 1954-56, 1973-74, & 2000.)

7) A – 1898 (The Sooners traveled to Fort Worth, Texas for a game vs. Fort Worth on November 28, 1898. This would also be their first out-of-state victory [Oklahoma 24, Fort Worth 0].)

8) D – OU has played all three (Oklahoma's record vs. U.S. Service Academies is: 1-0 vs. Air Force, 2-1 vs. Army, & 0-1 vs. Navy.)

9) A – True (1985 & 1986)

10) B – Iowa State (OU has played Iowa State a combined total 74 times through the 2007 season.)

11) A – .417 (OU's all-time record versus rival Texas is 40-57-5.)

12) C – Jason White (Jason had 383 yards on 35 of 29 passing in the 2004 season.)

13) B – 5 (Colorado in 1995, Nebraska in 2000, Kansas State in 2001, Oklahoma State in 2003, & Missouri in 2007.)

14) A – 1896 (OU defeated Norman High twice in 1896 to record their first winning [and undefeated] season.)

15) C – 65 (2003; Oklahoma 65, Texas 13)

16) D – Adrian Peterson (Adrian racked up 1,925 yards [148.1 average] in 2004.)

17) B – 16 (Oklahoma defeated Nebraska every season from 1943 through the 1958 season.)

18) C – 17-0 (In the 17 games played since 1901, Baylor has never beaten the Sooners.)

19) B – 2 (Billy Sims in 1980 and Lee Roy Selmon in 1976)

20) A – True (The Oklahoma Sooners have won 24 of their 41 total bowl games.)

21) C – 96 yards (Jeff Frazier vs. North Texas in 1995 and Buck McPhail vs. Kansas State in 1951)

22) B – Orange Bowl (1939; Tennessee 17, Oklahoma 0)

23) A – Rhodes Scholar (Jack Mildren was an Oklahoma quarterback and exceptional student from 1969-71.)

24) D – 18 (Oklahoma's first Orange Bowl appearance was in 1939 and their most recent was in 2005.)

25) C – 5 (Kurt Burris in 1954, Greg Pruitt in 1972, Billy Sims in 1979, Josh Heupel in 2000, and Adrian Peterson in 2004)

26) B – 1979 (OU was 10-4 on the season.)

27) C – 9 (The first season in which OU was ranked number one in the Preseason *AP* Poll was 1956 and the most recent occurrence was in 2003.)

28) A – True (OU has ended 30 seasons with 10 or more wins, which is 2 more than the second-best Alabama Crimson Tide.)

29) C – Jack Harts (1895 season)

30) A – 1 (Oklahoma was 0-1 in its inaugural season of college football.)

31) D – Malcolm Kelly (142 yards receiving vs. Nebraska in the 2006 season.)

32) A – 52 points (1978 vs. Rice)

33) C – De'Mond Parker (De'Mond rushed for 291 yards on 31 attempts vs. Texas in 1997.)

34) B – 179 points (179-0 vs. Kingfisher College in 1917.)

35) D – West Virginia (Fiesta Bowl; West Virginia 48, Oklahoma 28)

36) A – Washington (October 20, 1923; Oklahoma 62, Washington 7)

37) C – 4 (No school's players have won more. Brian Bosworth was honored with the award in its first two years, Rocky Calmus in 2001, and Teddy Lehman in 2003.)

38) B – 63 (Ranging from Roland "Waddy" Young in 1938 to Adrian Peterson in 2004.)

39) C – Josh Heupel (3,850 yards on 553 attempts and 349 completions in 1999)

40) A – True (Jason White in 2003)

41) B – Mark Clayton (Mark had 190 yards receiving vs. Texas in 2003.)

42) C – 26 (Ranging from Jerald Moore's 1,001 yards to Adrian Peterson's 1,925 yards.)

43) A – Zac Henderson (A two-time All-American defensive back, he earned consensus All-American in 1977.)

44) D – 41 (This includes Southwest Conference [2], Missouri Valley Conference [1], Big 6 Conference [6], Big 7 Conference [11], Big 8 Conference [16], and Big 12 Conference [5] Championships.)

45) D – None of the above (OU's football program does not retire jersey numbers.)

46) A – 54-2 (For a .964 winning percentage)

47) D – 18 (Ranging from Billy Vessels who was inducted in 1989 to Keith Jackson who was inducted in 2006.)

48) B – 1 (Coach Stoops was the recipient of the Paul "Bear" Bryant Award in 2000.)

49) A – 1950s (90% winning percentage for the decade under Coach Wilkinson.)

50) B – 14 (Ranging from Bob Warmack in 1968 to Torrance Marshall in 2001.)

Note: All answers valid as of the end of the 2007 season, unless otherwise indicated in the question itself.

1) What are the most yards rushing a Sooner has had in a bowl game?

    A) 212 yards
    B) 239 yards
    C) 247 yards
    D) 286 yards

2) What is the Oklahoma record for most tackles in a single game?

    A) 15
    B) 18
    C) 23
    D) 30

3) In which year was the first 10-win season at Oklahoma?

    A) 1899
    B) 1906
    C) 1911
    D) 1915

4) Which Sooner head coach has the second highest total wins in team history?

    A) Bud Wilkinson
    B) Bennie Owen
    C) Barry Switzer
    D) Bob Stoops

Third Quarter *3-Point Questions*

5) What was the largest margin of victory for Oklahoma in a bowl game?

    A) 27 points
    B) 34 points
    C) 35 points
    D) 37 points

6) Who holds the OU career record for receiving yards?

    A) Keith Jackson
    B) Mark Clayton
    C) Quentin Griffin
    D) Buster Rhymes

7) Which of the following Oklahoma QBs NEVER threw more than 20 touchdown passes in a single season?

    A) Nate Hybl
    B) Paul Thompson
    C) Jason White
    D) Cale Gundy

8) For all games played in 2007, in which quarter did the Sooners score the most points?

    A) First
    B) Second
    C) Third
    D) Fourth

9) Which of the following OU players has kicked 11 extra points in a single game?

    A) Tim Lashar
    B) Trey DiCarlo
    C) Both of the above
    D) None of the above

10) How many Sooners have won the Outland Trophy?

    A) 3
    B) 5
    C) 7
    D) 9

11) The Sooners have the best overall record in the nation since both World War II and the establishment of the *AP* Poll.

    A) True
    B) False

12) All-time, how many Sooners have been named First Team All-Conference?

    A) 165
    B) 249
    C) 372
    D) 428

13) Which Sooner holds the school record for the most rushes in a single game?

     A)   Adrian Peterson
     B)   Greg Pruitt
     C)   Steve Owens
     D)   Billy Sims

14) Who has the most career interceptions for Oklahoma?

     A)   J.T. Thatcher
     B)   Darrell Royal
     C)   Randy Hughes
     D)   Ricky Dixon

15) Which OU coach has had the best winning percentage?

     A)   Barry Switzer
     B)   Bob Stoops
     C)   Bud Wilkinson
     D)   Tom Stidham

16) Against which team was OU's team record for total offense set in 1980?

     A)   Kansas
     B)   Oklahoma State
     C)   Colorado
     D)   Baylor

17) In how many seasons has OU scored 600+ total points?

A) 0
B) 1
C) 11
D) 12

18) What is OU's record for most rushing yards in a game?

A) 501
B) 633
C) 692
D) 768

19) Which OU quarterback had 5 touchdown passes in his first career start?

A) Josh Heupel
B) Jason White
C) Eric Moore
D) Claude Arnold

20) What are the most passing yards for OU against Nebraska?

A) 287
B) 329
C) 383
D) 391

Third Quarter 3-Point Questions

SOONEROLOGY TRIVIA CHALLENGE

21) Which of the following OU quarterbacks had the highest career winning percentage?

    A) Steve Davis
    B) Jimmy Harris
    C) Darrell Royal
    D) Eddie Crowder

22) Which of the following OU head coaches played college football as a Sooner?

    A) John Blake
    B) Gary Gibbs
    C) Dewey Luster
    D) All of the above

23) Sooner legend Billy Sims recorded 200+ yard games eight times during his college career.

    A) True
    B) False

24) Who was the first consensus All-American wide receiver at Oklahoma?

    A) Albert Hall
    B) Ben Hart
    C) Mark Clayton
    D) None of the above

OKLAHOMA SOONERS FOOTBALL

25) Oklahoma is tied with Notre Dame for the most weeks ranked #1 in the *AP* Poll (including the preseason poll).

   A) True
   B) False

26) Who was the first consensus All-American linebacker at Oklahoma?

   A) Darrell Royal
   B) Rod Shoate
   C) Carl McAdams
   D) Daryl Hunt

27) In OU's 41 bowl appearances, how many times has a Sooner won bowl MVP (or MOP)?

   A) 7
   B) 18
   C) 23
   D) None of the above

28) Which Sooner WR holds the school record for yards per reception in a game?

   A) Mark Clayton
   B) Virgil Boll
   C) Trent Smith
   D) Jon Harrison

29) How many Oklahoma players have been named consensus All-Americans more than once?

   A) 6
   B) 11
   C) 14
   D) 17

30) Which of the following schools is not led by a former Stoops assistant coach?

   A) Kansas
   B) Nebraska
   C) Texas Tech
   D) Colorado

31) Against which team did OU get their first Big 12 win?

   A) Texas
   B) Kansas
   C) Oklahoma State
   D) Texas Tech

32) What is Oklahoma's longest drought between Bowl games since 1950?

   A) 4 years
   B) 5 years
   C) 6 years
   D) 7 years

33) Which of the following pairs include the Sooners' only two three-time All-Americans?

    A) Mark Hutson & Mark Clayton
    B) Buddy Burris & Rod Shoate
    C) Rocky Calmus & Dewey Selmon
    D) Steve Owens & Daryl Hunt

34) How did OU score its first points in the 2007 Big 12 Championship Game vs. #1 ranked Missouri?

    A) Punt return
    B) Field goal
    C) Pass
    D) Run

35) In 2007, Sooner QB Sam Bradford had a higher passing efficiency rating than Heisman winner Tim Tebow.

    A) True
    B) False

36) How many 100-yard games did Adrian Peterson have while at OU?

    A) 16
    B) 17
    C) 19
    D) 22

37) How many Sooners were drafted in the 1988 NFL Draft?

  A) 4
  B) 7
  C) 13
  D) 15

38) In how many televised games has OU played?

  A) 263
  B) 301
  C) 389
  D) 492

39) Which of the following school's current stadiums is larger than Memorial Stadium?

  A) Nebraska
  B) Auburn
  C) Notre Dame
  D) Texas

40) In 1995 did OU senior running back Jerald Moore have more or less than 1,000 yards rushing?

  A) More than 1,000 yards
  B) Less than 1,000 yards

Third Quarter   *3-Point Questions*

41) When was the last season the Sooners played the same school twice?

    A) 1998
    B) 2000
    C) 2002
    D) 2004

42) How many Oklahoma players have been drafted in the first round of the NFL Draft?

    A) 37
    B) 43
    C) 51
    D) None of the above

43) What position did Coach Stoops play in college?

    A) Full Back
    B) Defensive Line
    C) Tight End
    D) Defensive Back

44) Who coached Oklahoma in its first Big 12 Season?

    A) Howard Schnellenberger
    B) Bob Stoops
    C) John Blake
    D) Gary Gibbs

45) When is the next time OU is scheduled to play Notre Dame?

    A) 2010
    B) 2012
    C) 2013
    D) 2015

46) Did Quentin Griffin out rush the entire Florida State team in the 2000 National Championship game?

    A) Yes
    B) No

47) For whom is Owen Field named?

    A) Tinker Owen
    B) Bennie Owen
    C) Steve Owen
    D) Jim Owen

48) What is Oklahoma's longest drought between conference championships?

    A) 11 seasons
    B) 14 seasons
    C) 17 seasons
    D) 22 seasons

49) Did Billy Sims play in three consecutive Orange Bowls?

    A) Yes
    B) No

50) What are the most consecutive bowl losses by the Sooners?

    A) 1
    B) 2
    C) 5
    D) 6

Third Quarter Sooner Cool Fact

They perfected the 'bone. Many college football historians trace the birth of the wishbone formation back as far as the 1950s, but it was Oklahoma Head Coach Chuck Fairbanks and then Assistant Coach Barry Switzer who set in motion the machine that would perfect the offensive formation. With quarterback Jack Mildren under center, Switzer implemented the 'bone the fourth game of the 1970 season. Although Texas used the wishbone in winning the National Championship the previous year, it was Oklahoma's experimentation and use of the offense throughout the Switzer era that gave it its prominence in college football. Three National Championships, two undefeated seasons, twelve conference titles, eight bowl victories, and an impressive .837 winning percentage as head coach serve as witness to the perfecting of the 'bone during the Switzer era.

Third Quarter Answer Key

1) B – 239 yards (Marcus Dupree, 1983 Fiesta Bowl vs. Arizona State)

2) C – 23 (Jackie Shipp had 23 tackles vs. Mizzou in 1981.)

3) D – 1915 (OU was 10-0 including a SWC record of 3-0 in winning the conference title.)

4) A – Bud Wilkinson (Coach Wilkinson's overall record was 145-29-4 [.826].)

5) C – 35 points (Sugar Bowl, 1950 vs. LSU)

6) B – Mark Clayton (From 2000-04 Mark had 3,220 career yards receiving to set this Sooner record.)

7) D – Cale Gundy (The most TDs Cale threw was 17 as a senior in 1993.)

8) B – Second (First 129, Second 169, Third 135, and Fourth 159 for a total 592 points in 2007.)

9) C – Both of the above (Tim kicked 11 PATs vs. Mizzou in 1986 and Trey kicked 11 vs. Texas A&M in 2003.)

10) B – 5 (Jim Weatherall 1951, J.D. Roberts 1953, Lee Roy Selmon 1975, Greg Roberts 1978, and Jammal Brown 2004)

11) A – True (OU's record since 1936 [beginning of the *AP* Poll] is 592-192-22 [.749] and since 1946 is 535-163-13 [.762].)

12) D – 428 (At least one Sooner has been named first team all-conference in 92 of the 93 seasons OU has played as a member of a conference.)

13) C – Steve Owens (Steve had 55 rushes vs. Oklahoma State in 1969.)

14) B – Darrell Royal (Darrell pulled in a total of 18 interceptions in his career at OU [1946-49].)

15) A – Barry Switzer (Coach Switzer's overall record from 1973-88 was 157-29-4 [.837].)

16) C – Colorado (The Sooners had 875 yards of total offense in that game.)

17) B – 1 (In 2003 the Sooners scored a total of 601 points.)

18) D – 768 (A record set against Kansas State in 1988.)

19) A – Josh Heupel (1999 versus Indiana State)

20) C – 383 (This record was set in 2004.)

21) B – Jimmy Harris (From 1954-56 Jimmy was 25-0 as starting QB for OU. Gene Calame [not listed as a multiple choice option was also .1000 [15-0].)

22) D – All of the above (John Blake from 1979-82, Gary Gibbs from 1972-74, and Dewey Luster from 1917-1920)

23) B – False (He recorded 7, a record which still stands today.)

24) D – None of the above (Mark Clayton is a two-time All-American WR for OU, with neither selection being consensus.)

25) A – True (The Sooners and Irish are tied at 95 weeks all-time at #1 in the *AP* Poll.)

26) C – Carl McAdams (Carl received his first All-American selection in 1964 and a consensus selection in 1965.)

27) A – 7 (Leon Heath in the 1950 Sugar Bowl, Jack Mildren in the 1970 Bluebonnet Bowl, Derrick Sheppard in the 1981 Sun Bowl, Cale Gundy in the 1991 Gator Bowl & 1993 John Hancock Bowl, Torrance Marshall in the 2001 Orange Bowl, and Nate Hybl in the 2003 Rose Bowl)

28) B – Virgil Boll (47.7 yards per reception [3-143] vs. Colorado in 1962)

29) C – 14 (Ranging from Jim Weatherall in 1950-51 to Tommy Harris in 2002-03)

30) D – Colorado (Mark Mangino – Kansas, Mike Leach – Texas Tech, and Bo Pelini – Nebraska)

31) A – Texas (On October 12, 1996 OU defeated Texas 30-27 in OT to claim its first Big 12 victory of inaugural Big 12 Season.)

32) B – 5 years (Following OU's 6-31 loss vs. BYU in the 1994 Copper Bowl, the Sooners did not play in another bowl game until the 1999 Independence Bowl.)

33) B – Buddy Burris & Rod Shoate (Buddy from 1946-48 and Rod from 1972-1974)

34) D – Run (A 3-yard run by Chris Brown in the second quarter.)

35) A – True (Sam led the nation [176.53 rating] ahead of Tim Tebow [172.5 rating].)

36) D – 22 (Ranging from his exact 100-yard performance vs. Bowling Green in 2004 to his 249-yard personal best vs. Oklahoma State in 2004)

37) C – 13 (It's the most players the Sooners have had drafted in a single draft.)

38) A – 263 (The Sooners are 171-87-5 all-time in televised games.)

39) B – Auburn (Auburn's Jordan-Hare Stadium's capacity is only 5,339 seats higher than Oklahoma Memorial Stadium.)

40) A – More than 1,000 yards (Jerald had 1,001 yards.)

41) C – 2002 (OU defeated Colorado once in conference play [27-11] and once in the Big 12 Championship Game [29-7].)

42) A – 37 (No Sooners were selected in the first round of the 2008 draft, making Adrian Peterson [2007 draft] the most recent OU player to be drafted in the first round.)

43) D – Defensive Back (University of Iowa 1979-82)

44) C – John Blake (3-8 in the Big 12's inaugural season)

45) B – 2012 (OU is scheduled to take on the Golden Domers two consecutive seasons starting in 2012.)

46) A – Yes (Quentin gained 40 yards rushing on 11 attempts compared to the Seminoles' team total 27 yards on 17 carries.)

47) B – Bennie Owen (Coach Owen led the Sooners from 1905-1926. Tinker, Steve, and Jim were all OU All-Americans but their last names were Owens [not Owen].)

48) C – 17 seasons (In each season from 1921-37 OU did not win a conference title.)

49) A – Yes (A 1978 loss to Arkansas [31-6], a 1979 victory over Nebraska [31-24], and a 1980 victory over Florida State [24-7])

50) B – 2 (In its 41 bowl appearances, OU has never lost more than two bowl games in a row. Back to back losses have happened on six occasions and on one occasion a loss was followed by a tie.)

Note: All answers valid as of the end of the 2007 season, unless otherwise indicated in the question itself.

Fourth Quarter *4-Point Questions*

1) Which of the following Big 12 schools has more players in the College Football Hall of Fame than OU?

   A) Nebraska
   B) Texas
   C) Both of the above
   D) None of the above

2) Of the following Oklahoma opponents, which is the only one the Sooners HAVE beaten?

   A) Mississippi
   B) Iowa
   C) BYU
   D) Arizona State

3) What was the first year 80,000 fans attended an Oklahoma-Texas game?

   A) 1950
   B) 1976
   C) 1992
   D) 2007

4) The Sooners have lost every game in which they allowed their opponent to score 50 or more points.

   A) True
   B) False

Fourth Quarter *4-Point Questions*

5) Which kicker had the most points for Oklahoma in a single game against Texas?

   A) Uve von Schamann
   B) Tim Duncan
   C) R.D. Lashar
   D) Trey DiCarlo

6) Against which conference does OU have the second most all-time victories?

   A) ACC
   B) Conference USA
   C) Pac 10
   D) Big East

7) What is the largest crowd to have ever watched a Sooners bowl game?

   A) 79,604
   B) 81,775
   C) 86,848
   D) 103,126

8) How many Oklahoma coaches are in the College Football Hall of Fame?

   A) 2
   B) 3
   C) 4
   D) 5

Fourth Quarter *4-Point Questions*

9) Of the following Oklahoma opponents, which is the only team the Sooners HAVE NOT beaten?

 A) Duke
 B) Boise State
 C) LSU
 D) Ohio State

10) Which of the following OU coaches is the only one to lead his teams to bowl games in his first nine seasons?

 A) Bob Stoops
 B) Bennie Owen
 C) Barry Switzer
 D) Bud Wilkinson

11) Currently, for how many consecutive years has OU had a player drafted in the NFL Draft?

 A) 16
 B) 28
 C) 31
 D) 46

12) What are the fewest rushing yards allowed by OU in a game?

 A) -79
 B) -52
 C) -34
 D) -15

Fourth Quarter *4-Point Questions*

13) Which of the following Big 12 opponents averaged more points per game in 2007 than the Sooners?

  A) Kansas
  B) Texas Tech
  C) Missouri
  D) Texas

14) Who holds the Oklahoma single season rushing record?

  A) Billy Sims
  B) Joe Washington
  C) Adrian Peterson
  D) Marcus Dupree

15) When was the last time the Sooners were shutout?

  A) 1989
  B) 1991
  C) 1995
  D) 1998

16) OU has played more than or less than 200 total games versus teams located within the State of Oklahoma?

  A) More than 200 games
  B) Less than 200 games

Fourth Quarter *4-Point Questions*

17) Who was the Sooners' first African-American All-American?

  A) Lee Roy Selmon
  B) Dewey Selmon
  C) Granville Liggins
  D) Terry Webb

18) What are the fewest TDs OU has allowed in a season?

  A) 0
  B) 4
  C) 12
  D) 19

19) Who holds the OU record for rushing TDs in a career and co-holds the record for rushing TDs in a season?

  A) Steve Owens
  B) Billy Sims
  C) Quentin Griffin
  D) Adrian Peterson

20) Who are the only two Sooner QBs to hold four of the team's top-50 records for passing yards in a season?

  A) Steve Davis & Eddie Crowder
  B) Jack Mildren & Bob Warmack
  C) Josh Heupel & Jason White
  D) Cale Gundy & Jamelle Holieway

Fourth Quarter   *4-Point Questions*

21) How many total head coaches has Oklahoma had?

A) 17
B) 21
C) 24
D) 28

22) What is the largest margin of victory for Oklahoma against Texas?

A) 30 points
B) 41 points
C) 52 points
D) 63 points

23) Which Sooners head coach has the second best winning percentage?

A) Bob Stoops
B) Tom Stidham
C) Vernon Parrington
D) Bud Wilkinson

24) Has Oklahoma played every Pac 10 team at least once?

A) Yes
B) No

Fourth Quarter *4-Point Questions*

25) What on-campus organization represents OU in the exchange of the Red River Rivalry Trophy with Texas?

   A) Athletic Department
   B) Band
   C) Student Government
   D) Lettermen's Society

26) Against which BCS Conference does Oklahoma have the worst winning percentage?

   A) ACC
   B) Pac 10
   C) Big East
   D) SEC

27) Approximately how many Pride of Oklahoma Band members take the field during OU football games?

   A) 250
   B) 300
   C) 350
   D) 400

28) How many Oklahoma coaches have won a National Coach of the Year award while at OU?

   A) 0
   B) 1
   C) 2
   D) 3

Fourth Quarter *4-Point Questions*

29) What decade did Oklahoma have its worst winning percentage?

   A) 1920s
   B) 1930s
   C) 1980s
   D) 1990s

30) The Sooners surpassed 800 overall wins in the 2007 season.

   A) True
   B) False

31) How many of OU's 144 All-Americans do not have known jersey numbers?

   A) 0
   B) 1
   C) 7
   D) 8

32) Which BCS Conference was the Sooners' most recent bowl opponent from?

   A) Big East
   B) ACC
   C) SEC
   D) Big Ten

33) When was the last time the Sooners scored on a safety?

A) 2004
B) 2005
C) 2006
D) 2007

34) What was the worst defeat Oklahoma suffered in a bowl game?

A) 27 points
B) 36 points
C) 44 points
D) 51 points

35) Which Sooner holds the Orange Bowl record for most solo tackles?

A) Jackie Shipp
B) Rocky Calmus
C) Brian Bosworth
D) Daryl Hunt

36) How many times has Oklahoma appeared in the Orange/Sugar/Fiesta/Gator bowls combined?

A) 27
B) 29
C) 30
D) 31

Fourth Quarter *4-Point Questions*

37) Who is the only Sooner to have won the Mosi Tatupu Award?

   A) Jarrail Jackson
   B) Brandon Daniels
   C) J.T. Thatcher
   D) No Sooner has won the award

38) Who was the first consensus All-American lineman at Oklahoma?

   A) Gilford Duggan
   B) Buddy Burris
   C) John Rapacz
   D) Roy Smoot

39) Adrian Peterson is the current holder of which of the following BCS Championship Game records?

   A) Most Rushing Yards
   B) Most Total Yards
   C) Most Rushing Attempts
   D) All of the above

40) Every 300+ yard passing game by a Sooner quarterback has taken place since 1980.

   A) True
   B) False

Fourth Quarter *4-Point Questions*

41) Which Oklahoma Heisman Trophy winner was drafted highest in the NFL Draft?

    A) Steve Owens
    B) Billy Vessels
    C) Jason White
    D) Billy Sims

42) How many OU players have won the Lombardi Award?

    A) 3
    B) 4
    C) 5
    D) 6

43) What is the name of the honorary site where bronze statues of Sooner Heisman winners can be found?

    A) Sooner Hall of Fame
    B) Heisman Park
    C) Oklahoma Athletic Hall of Fame
    D) The Row

44) What was the best winning percentage of an Oklahoma head coach who lasted only one season?

    A) 50%
    B) 60%
    C) 72.7%
    D) 80%

Fourth Quarter   *4-Point Questions*

45) When was the last time the Sooners shutout an opponent?

   A)   2000
   B)   2002
   C)   2004
   D)   2006

46) As of the end of the 2007 season, how many Sooners played in the NFL?

   A)   22
   B)   24
   C)   25
   D)   27

47) Oklahoma led the nation in which of the following statistical categories in 2007?

   A)   Punt Returns & Pass Defense
   B)   Kickoff Returns & Passing Efficiency
   C)   Scoring Offense & Sacks Allowed
   D)   Passing Efficiency & Total Defense

48) What are the fewest wins OU has had in a single season (minimum 8 games)?

   A)   1
   B)   2
   C)   3
   D)   4

Fourth Quarter   *4-Point Questions*

SOONEROLOGY TRIVIA CHALLENGE

49) How many returns for touchdowns in a single game did OU have in setting the current NCAA record?

    A) 3
    B) 4
    C) 5
    D) 6

50) Since the end of World War II, the Sooners have led which of the following categories?

    A) Victories & Winning Percentage
    B) Weeks Ranked #1 & in the Top 5 of the *AP* Poll
    C) Points Scored & Weeks Ranked #1 in the BCS
    D) All of the above

OKLAHOMA SOONERS FOOTBALL

Fourth Quarter Sooner Cool Fact

At the mid-point of the 2000 college football season, Oklahoma proved once again that an *AP* national ranking does not guarantee victory over the Crimson and Cream. In a month which will forever be known as Red October, OU prepared for battle against #2 ranked Kansas State and #1 ranked Nebraska by way of a 63-14 route of favored rival Texas on October 7th. One Week later the Sooners would face K-State and roll to a 41-31 victory handing the Wildcats their first loss of the season. Following a bye week, the Sooners were set to face the #1-ranked Cornhuskers at home. With ESPN's *College GameDay* on location, the Crimson and Cream toppled the Huskers 31-14 in front of 75,000+ fans. This marked the first time in NCAA history that #1 and #2 *AP*-ranked teams were defeated in successive weeks by the same team. Of course OU would go on to hold the #1 ranking too and when it mattered the most – in the final poll. The 13-0 Sooners brought home their 7th National Championship amid the wintry white of January.

Fourth Quarter Answer Key

1) D – None of the above (OU has 18 players in the Hall, Nebraska has 13, and Texas has 14.)

2) B – Iowa (OU is 1-0 vs. Iowa, 0-1 vs. Arizona State, 0-1 vs. BYU, and 0-1 vs. Mississippi.)

3) D – 2007 (Official attendance for the 2007 Red River Rivalry game is exactly 80,000. No previous season's game attendance officially exceeds it.)

4) A – True (All-time this has happened on 7 occasions and coincidentally, 3 of them were in 1996 and two of them in 1997.)

5) D – Trey DiCarlo (Trey had 17 points vs. Texas in 2003. Oklahoma 65, Texas 13)

6) B – Conference USA (The Sooners are 32-8 [.800] vs. Conference USA teams through the 2007 season.)

7) C – 86,848 (2003 Rose Bowl, Pasadena, California; Oklahoma 34, Washington State 14)

8) D – 5 (Benny Owen inducted 1951, Lawrence Jones inducted 1954, Bud Wilkinson inducted 1969, Jim Tatum inducted 1984, and Barry Switzer inducted 2001.)

9) B – Boise State (OU is 0-1 vs. Boise State, 1-0 vs. Duke, 1-2 vs. LSU, and 1-1 vs. Ohio State.)

10) A – Bob Stoops (1999-2007; previously not a single OU head coach had managed to take more than their first two teams to bowl games.)

11) D – 46 (From 1963-2008 at least one Sooner has been drafted in at least one of the rounds of the draft.)

12) B – -52 (In 1986 vs. Kansas)

13) A – Kansas (In 12 games Kansas averaged 44.3 points/game. In 13 games OU averaged 43.4.)

14) C – Adrian Peterson (1,925 yards in 2004)

15) D – 1998 (Oklahoma 0, Texas A&M 29; at College Station, TX)

16) A – More than 200 games (OU's all-time record vs. Oklahoma-based teams is 160-28-14 [202 total games].)

17) C – Granville Liggins (Granville was a two-time All-American in 1966-67 – consensus in 1967.)

18) B – 4 (In 1939 the Sooners shutout 9 of their 11 opponents.)

19) A – Steve Owens (Steve had 57 rushing TDs in his career [1967-69] and 23 rushing TDs in 1969, a record he co-holds with Billy Sims [1979].)

20) D – Cale Gundy & Jamelle Holieway (Cale holds the records for the 1990-93 seasons and Jamelle holds each of the season records for 1985-88.)

21) B – 21 (Bob Stoops is the 21st OU head coach.)

22) C – 52 points (On October 11, 2003 OU defeated Texas 65-13 edging out their previously highest margin of victory of 50 points over the Longhorns.)

23) D – Bud Wilkinson (Coach Wilkinson was 145-29-4 [.826] from 1947-1963. Coach Stoops current record of 97-22 [.820] is threatening to overtake second in this category.)

24) A – Yes (1-1 vs. Arizona, 0-1 vs. Arizona State, 2-2 vs. Cal, 6-1 vs. Oregon, 1-1 vs. Oregon State, 2-6 vs. Southern Cal, 3-1 vs. Stanford, 3-1 vs. UCLA, 1-1 vs. Washington, and 3-0 vs. Washington State)

25) C – Student Government (The Red River Rivalry Trophy has been passed back and forth between the school's student governments since 2003.)

26) B – Pac 10 (22-15-1 [.592] all-time)

27) B – 300 (The 300-piece band marches onto the field to the drummers' cadence just prior to kickoff.)

28) C – 2 (Barry Switzer: 1974 Walter Camp Coach of the Year Award and Bob Stoops: 2000 Paul "Bear" Bryant Award, 2000 Home Depot Coach of the Year Award, 2003 Bobby Dodd Coach of the Year Award, 2000 & 2003 Walter Camp Coach of the Year Award, and the 2000 Eddie Robinson Coach of the Year Award)

29) D – 1990s (OU was 61-51-3 for a winning percentage of .543 through the decade of the 1990s)

30) B – False (The Sooners have won a total of 779 football games in their team history.)

31) D – 8 (Claude Reeds [1913], Forest Geyer [1915], Phil White [1920], Roy Smoot [1920], Granville Norris [1927], Cash Gentry [1934], John Rapacz [1946], and Wade Walker [1949])

32) A – Big East (West Virginia joined the Big East in 1995. All-time OU is 18-3-1 vs. Big East schools.)

33) D – 2007 (Defensive end Alan Davis recorded a safety vs. North Texas in OU's 2007 season-opener on September 1, 2007.)

34) B – 36 points (In the 2005 Orange Bowl, Southern Cal took advantage of five Sooner turnovers in winning the BCS National Championship 55-19.)

35) C – Brian Bosworth (The Bos recorded 13 solo tackles vs. Penn State in the 1986 Orange Bowl.)

36) D – 31 (OU has appeared in 18 Orange Bowls, 6 Sugar Bowls, 4 Fiesta Bowls, and 3 Gator Bowls.)

37) C – J.T. Thatcher (Given to the Special Teams Player of the Year, J.T. won the award in 2000.)

38) B – Buddy Burris (Although other Sooner linemen received All-American honors prior to Buddy, he was the first lineman to receive Consensus All-American [1948], which was the same year in which he became the first 3-time All-American for the university.)

39) C – Most Rushing Attempts (Adrian had 25 attempts for 82 yards vs. Southern Cal on January 4, 2005.)

40) A – True (In fact, of the 32 games with 300 or more yards passing, all of them have taken place since 1991.)

41) D – Billy Sims (Billy Sims was the #1 overall draft pick in 1980, Billy Vessels was the #2 overall pick in 1953, Steve Owens was the #19 overall pick of the 1970 draft, and Jason White was undrafted in 2005.)

42) A – 3 (Lee Roy Selmon in 1975, Tony Casillas in 1985, and Tommie Harris in 2003)

43) B – Heisman Park (Located east of Owen Field, are bronze commemorative statues of Steve Owens, Billy Vessels, Billy Sims, and Jason White, all of which were sculpted by Oklahoma artists.)

44) C – 72.7% (Jim Tatum led the Sooners to an 8-3 record in his only year as head coach.)

45) D – 2006 (OU defeated Middle Tennessee 59-0 on September 23, 2006.)

46) C – 25 (Ranging from Kelly Gregg with 8 years in the league to numerous first-year players.)

47) B – Kickoff Returns & Passing Efficiency (The Sooners averaged 28.27 yards per kickoff return to lead all 119 FBS programs. Sooner passers had a 170.63 passing efficiency rating [Sam Bradford was 176.53 by himself] to lead the nation.)

48) B – 2 (In 1922 and 1924 Bennie Owen led the Sooners in seasons in which the team only managed to win two out of eight games.)

49) A – 3 (Oklahoma had 3 returns for touchdowns vs. UCLA on September 20, 2003.)

50) D – All of the above (OU has had phenomenal success since the end of the Second World War. They have had 535 victories, a .762 winning percentage, 95 weeks ranked #1 in the *AP* Poll, 352 weeks ranked in the Top 5 of the *AP* Poll, and 18 weeks ranked #1 in the BCS.)

Note: All answers valid as of the end of the 2007 season, unless otherwise indicated in the question itself.

Overtime Bonus *4-Point Questions*

1) Which coach has the second longest coaching tenure at Oklahoma?

   A) Barry Switzer
   B) Bob Stoops
   C) Chuck Fairbanks
   D) Bud Wilkinson

2) What is the longest winning streak for the Sooners in the Oklahoma-Texas series?

   A) 5
   B) 6
   C) 7
   D) 8

3) Which Oklahoma running back WAS NOT picked in the first round of the NFL Draft?

   A) Elvis Peacock
   B) Jermaine Fazande
   C) Steve Sewell
   D) David Overstreet

4) Oklahoma has had more players drafted number one overall in the NFL Draft than Oklahoma State.

   A) True
   B) False

Overtime Bonus *4-Point Questions*

5) How many times has a number one-ranked OU lost in a bowl game?

    A) 0
    B) 1
    C) 2
    D) 3

6) Oklahoma has scored more points in its program history than any other program?

    A) True
    B) False

7) How many conference wins did Coach Switzer have at OU?

    A) 80
    B) 85
    C) 95
    D) 100

8) How many Oklahoma players had over 100 tackles in 2007?

    A) 0
    B) 1
    C) 2
    D) 3

Overtime Bonus *4-Point Questions*

9) What is the Sooners' longest streak of weeks ranked in the *AP* Poll?

    A)   129
    B)   138
    C)   141
    D)   158

10) In 1917 Oklahoma scored 179 points, the school record for most points in a game, versus Kingfisher College, which university is Kingfisher now a part of?

    A)   Nebraska
    B)   Texas
    C)   Oklahoma State
    D)   None of the above

Overtime Bonus Answer Key

1) D – Bud Wilkinson (17 seasons [1947-63], which just edges out Coach Switzer's 16 seasons [1973-88].)

2) B – 6 (OU defeated Texas in each Red River Rivalry Game from 1952-1957.)

3) B – Jermaine Fazande (Jermaine, 2nd round pick in 1999; Sewell, 1st round pick in 1985; Overstreet, 1st round pick in 1981; and Peacock, 1st round pick in 1978)

4) A – True (OU has had two overall number one draft picks to OSU's one.)

5) C – 2 (1988 Orange Bowl [OU 14, Miami 20] and 1951 Sugar Bowl [OU 7, Kentucky 13])

6) A – True (29,772 points; Michigan [29,347] and Nebraska [29,124] round out the top three.)

7) D – 100 (This is the most by any OU head coach.)

8) B – 1 (Curtis Lofton had 157 total tackles in 2007.)

9) D – 158 (From the 12th week of 1970 to the 5th week of 1981)

10) D – None of the above (Kingfisher College was absorbed by the University of Oklahoma in 1927.)

Note: All answers valid as of the end of the 2007 season, unless otherwise indicated in the question itself.

Player / Team Score Sheet

Name:_____

First Quarter			Second Quarter			Third Quarter			Fourth Quarter			Overtime	
1	26		1	26		1	26		1	26		1	
2	27		2	27		2	27		2	27		2	
3	28		3	28		3	28		3	28		3	
4	29		4	29		4	29		4	29		4	
5	30		5	30		5	30		5	30		5	
6	31		6	31		6	31		6	31		6	
7	32		7	32		7	32		7	32		7	
8	33		8	33		8	33		8	33		8	
9	34		9	34		9	34		9	34		9	
10	35		10	35		10	35		10	35		10	
11	36		11	36		11	36		11	36			
12	37		12	37		12	37		12	37			
13	38		13	38		13	38		13	38			
14	39		14	39		14	39		14	39			
15	40		15	40		15	40		15	40			
16	41		16	41		16	41		16	41			
17	42		17	42		17	42		17	42			
18	43		18	43		18	43		18	43			
19	44		19	44		19	44		19	44			
20	45		20	45		20	45		20	45			
21	46		21	46		21	46		21	46			
22	47		22	47		22	47		22	47			
23	48		23	48		23	48		23	48			
24	49		24	49		24	49		24	49			
25	50		25	50		25	50		25	50			
___ x 1 = ___			___ x 2 = ___			___ x 3 = ___			___ x 4 = ___			___ x 4 = ___	

Multiply total number correct by point value/quarter to calculate totals for each quarter.

Add total of all quarters below.

Total Points:_____

Thank you for playing Soonerology Trivia Challenge.

Additional score sheets are available at:
www.TriviaGameBooks.com

Player / Team Score Sheet

SOONEROLOGY TRIVIA CHALLENGE

Name:_____

First Quarter			Second Quarter			Third Quarter			Fourth Quarter			Overtime	
1	26		1	26		1	26		1	26		1	
2	27		2	27		2	27		2	27		2	
3	28		3	28		3	28		3	28		3	
4	29		4	29		4	29		4	29		4	
5	30		5	30		5	30		5	30		5	
6	31		6	31		6	31		6	31		6	
7	32		7	32		7	32		7	32		7	
8	33		8	33		8	33		8	33		8	
9	34		9	34		9	34		9	34		9	
10	35		10	35		10	35		10	35		10	
11	36		11	36		11	36		11	36			
12	37		12	37		12	37		12	37			
13	38		13	38		13	38		13	38			
14	39		14	39		14	39		14	39			
15	40		15	40		15	40		15	40			
16	41		16	41		16	41		16	41			
17	42		17	42		17	42		17	42			
18	43		18	43		18	43		18	43			
19	44		19	44		19	44		19	44			
20	45		20	45		20	45		20	45			
21	46		21	46		21	46		21	46			
22	47		22	47		22	47		22	47			
23	48		23	48		23	48		23	48			
24	49		24	49		24	49		24	49			
25	50		25	50		25	50		25	50			
___ x 1 =___			___ x 2 =___			___ x 3 =___			___ x 4 =___			___ x 4 =___	

Multiply total number correct by point value/quarter to calculate totals for each quarter.

Add total of all quarters below.

Total Points:_____

Thank you for playing Soonerology Trivia Challenge.

Additional score sheets are available at:
www.TriviaGameBooks.com